End Times

The Lutheran Difference Series

Mark Brighton

Written by Mark Brighton

Edited by Tom Doyle and Edward Engelbrecht

This publication is available in braille and in large print for the visually impaired. Write to the Library for the Blind, 1333 S. Kirkwood Road, St. Louis, MO 63122-7295; or call 1-800-433-3954.

1 2 3 4 5 6 7 8 9 10   10 09 08 07 06 05 04 03 02 01

Contents

About This Series

"Pastor, it was so nice of you to visit."

"Happy to stop by."

"I have a question for you. You know my son, Bob, don't you?"

"Yes, he's away at college."

"That's right. Well, he visited last week with his girlfriend, Tammy. They announced that they are engaged."

"Congratulations!"

"Yes, Tammy's so nice. But I was wondering . . . she's Baptist and we're Lutheran. I know Tammy's a Christian, but what do Baptists believe? How are Lutherans different?"

As Lutherans interact with other Christians, they often find themselves struggling to explain their beliefs and practices. Although many Lutherans have learned the "what" of the doctrines of the church, they do not always have a full scriptural foundation to share the "why." When confronted with different doctrines, they cannot clearly state their faith, much less understand the differences between denominations.

Because of insecurities about explaining particular doctrines or practices, some Lutherans may avoid opportunities to share what they have learned from Christ and His Word. The Lutheran Difference Bible study series will identify how Lutherans differ from other Christians and demonstrate from the Bible why Lutherans differ. These studies will prepare Lutherans to share their faith and help non-Lutherans understand the Lutheran difference.

Student Introduction

"Anita, I'm so excited! I just came from the John Thompson Bible Prophecy Conference."

"Who's John Thompson?"

"What? *You* haven't heard about Dr. John Thompson, today's leading Bible prophecy expert? I have all his books, and it was such an honor to hear him speak."

"Really? I guess I don't know that much about Bible prophecy."

"Let me show you what I've learned about the Book of Revelation . . ."

In *Doomsday: The End of the World—a View through Time*, Russell Chandler describes the research of Jon Stone, a professor of religion who has made a list of books published about the end times. After listing 2,100 titles, Stone realized that only 50 books were written by Roman Catholic or mainline Protestant authors! The other 2,050 titles on his list vividly demonstrate the fascination and obsession that American evangelicals (mostly Baptists, Anabaptists, and Pentecostals) have with the end times.

In contrast to the interests of American evangelicals, this Bible study does not even begin with the end times. It begins with the personal end that each person faces—death. Lutherans have traditionally started their study of the second coming of Christ, His final judgment, and heaven and hell with the topic of death because until Christ returns, that's how we will enter the end times. This represents a different approach from most Christian teaching. Instead of waiting for the coming reign of Christ, Lutherans focus on living in Christ now through the Holy Spirit's work.

Prophecy Buffs

In recent years, Hal Lindsey's *The Late Great Planet Earth* and Tim LaHaye and Jerry Jenkins's fictional *Left Behind* series have made a narrow focus on the end times immensely popular. In some evangelical congregations, the preaching and teaching focus on virtually no other subject. Prophecy teachers compete to provide the latest theory so they can gain a cut of the end-times market share. As a result, historical perspective gets left behind.

For example, few laypeople who believe in the rapture realize that this doctrine first appeared in the 1830s. It had never been taught among Christians before! A pastor named John Nelson Darby popularized the rapture theory nearly 1,800 years after Christ taught the disciples about His reappearing. Yet today many Christians assume that the rapture doctrine is a long-standing interpretation of the Bible.

The Lutheran reformers had a different, simpler understanding of the end times and the focus of Christian teaching. The following charts will help you compare and contrast the two most widely held views of the end times.

Premillennialism

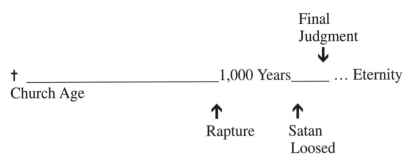

Amillennialism

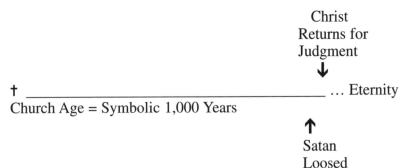

Premill and Amill

Chart 1 illustrates the commonly held beliefs of a premillennial understanding of the end times. According to this view, at some point in the future Christ will return and believers who are alive will meet Him in the air and be taken to heaven. Immediately afterward, a seven-year period of tribulation will commence for those upon the earth. During this tribulation, the Antichrist will appear. Then Christ will return again to establish a politically powerful and glorious kingdom upon earth, which will last 1,000 years. During this time Satan will be bound and certain martyred saints will be resurrected to reign with Christ on earth. At the conclusion of the 1,000 years, Satan will lead the nations in one last battle against God's people, the battle of Armageddon. Christ will defeat the devil and pronounce final judgment.

Note that according to this schema, Christ will return twice (for the rapture and the second judgment) and raise the dead twice. Then He will establish a glorious and politically powerful kingdom upon earth.

Depicted on chart 2, the alternative view, which aligns itself with early Christianity and Reformation theology, is that Christ's victory on the cross defeated and bound Satan. The reign of Christ, or the "millennium," has already commenced. During the millennium, which corresponds to the Church Age, the people of Christ reign with Him upon the earth. Yet this is no age of heaven upon earth, because Christ's victorious saints still fight against evil, including what St. John calls "the spirit of Antichrist." When God has accomplished His gracious purposes in Christ, Satan will be loosed, at which time the full embodiment of rebellion, the Antichrist, will appear. Satan's rebellion will be shortened by Christ's glorious return. Then all the dead will rise for Judgment Day.

This view of the end times, called amillennialism, has only one raising of the dead and one return of Christ. It discourages us from hoping for any glorious and politically powerful "heaven upon earth" in the millennium. This view is much simpler than premillennialism and fits with the Bible and early Christian teaching as recorded in the Apostles' Creed.

It goes beyond the scope of this study to treat all the significant differences and underlying theological ideas that support these two views. For an in-depth and scholarly treatment of this subject, look to Louis Brighton's commentary on Revelation, published by CPH. The discerning reader will quickly realize the depth of my indebtedness to the author of this popular commentary.

An Overview of Christian Denominations

The following outline of Christian history will help you understand where the different denominations come from and how they are related to one another. Use this outline in connection with the "Comparisons" sections found throughout the study. Statements of belief for the different churches are drawn from their official confessional writings.

The Great Schism

Eastern Orthodox: On July 16, 1054, Cardinal Humbert entered the Cathedral of the Holy Wisdom in Constantinople just before the worship service. He stepped to the altar and left a letter condemning Michael Cerularius, patriarch of Constantinople. Cerularius responded by condemning the letter and its authors. In that moment, Christian churches of the east and west were severed from one another. Their disagreements centered on what bread could be used in the Lord's Supper and the addition of the filioque statement to the Nicene Creed.

The Reformation

Lutheran: On June 15, 1520, Pope Leo X wrote a letter condemning Dr. Martin Luther for his Ninety-Five Theses. Luther's theses had challenged the sale of indulgences, a fund-raising effort to pay for the building of St. Peter's Cathedral in Rome. The letter charged Luther with heresy and threatened to excommunicate him if he did not retract his writings within 60 days. Luther replied by publicly burning the letter. Leo excommunicated him on January 3 and condemned all who agreed with Luther or supported his cause.

Reformed: In 1522 the preaching of Ulrich Zwingli in Zurich, Switzerland, convinced people to break their traditional Lenten fast. Also, Zwingli preached that priests should be allowed to marry. When local friars challenged these departures from medieval church practice, the Zurich Council supported Zwingli and agreed that the Bible should guide Christian doctrine and practice. Churches of this Reformed tradition include Presbyterians and Episcopalians.

Anabaptist: In January 1525 Conrad Grebel, a follower of Ulrich Zwingli, rebaptized Georg Blaurock. Blaurock began rebaptizing others and founded the Swiss Brethren. Their insistence on adult believers' Baptism distinguished them from other churches of the Reformation. Anabaptists attracted social extremists who advocated violence in the cause of Christ, complete pacifism, or communal living. Mennonite, Brethren, and Amish churches descend from this movement.

The Counter Reformation

Roman Catholic: When people call the medieval church "Roman Catholic," they make a common historical mistake. Roman Catholicism as we know it emerged after the Reformation. As early as 1518 Luther and other reformers had appealed to the pope and requested a council to settle the issue of indulgences. Their requests were hindered or denied for a variety of theological and political reasons. Finally, on December 13, 1545, 34 leaders from the churches who opposed the Reformation gathered at the invitation of Pope Paul III. They began the Council of Trent (1545–1563), which established the doctrine and practice of Roman Catholicism.

Post-Reformation Movements

Baptist: In 1608 or 1609 John Smyth, a former pastor of the Church of England, baptized himself by pouring water over his head. He formed a congregation of English Separatists in Holland, who opposed the rule of bishops and infant Baptism. This marked the start of the English Baptist churches, which remain divided doctrinally over the theology of **John Calvin** (Particular Baptists) and **Jacob Arminius** (General Baptists). In the 1800s the Restoration Movement of **Alexander Campbell**, a former Presbyterian minister, adopted many Baptist teachings. These churches include the Disciples of Christ (Christian Churches) and the Churches of Christ.

Wesleyan: In 1729 John and Charles Wesley gathered with three other men to study the Scripture, receive Communion, and discipline one another according to the "method" laid down in the Bible. Later, John Wesley's preaching caused religious revivals in England and America. Methodists, Wesleyans, Nazarenes, and Pentecostals form the Wesleyan family of churches.

Liberal: In 1799 Friedrich Schleiermacher published *Addresses on Religion* in an attempt to make Christianity appealing to people influenced by rationalism. He argued that religion is not a body of doctrines, provable truths, or a system of ethics, but belongs to the realm of feelings. His ideas did not lead to the formation of a new denomination, but deeply influenced Christian thinking. Denominations most thoroughly affected by liberalism are the United Church of Christ, Disciples of Christ, and Unitarianism.

Lutheran Facts

Lutheran churches first described themselves as *evangelische*, or evangelical, churches. Opponents of these churches called them *Lutheran* after Dr. Martin Luther, the sixteenth-century German church reformer.

Lutherans are not disciples of Dr. Martin Luther, but rather are disciples of Jesus Christ. They proudly accept the name *Lutheran* because they agree with Dr. Luther's teaching from the Bible, as summarized in Luther's Small Catechism.

All who worship the Holy Trinity and trust in Jesus Christ for the forgiveness of sins are regarded by Lutherans as fellow Christians, despite denominational differences.

Although all Christian churches use the Holy Scripture, Lutherans emphasize that the Scripture is the final and only certain judge of doctrine and practice (*sola scriptura*)—not human traditions, reason, or churchly authority.

Lutherans confess the three ecumenical creeds (Apostles', Nicene, and Athanasian) as correct summaries of biblical teaching.

Lutherans form the largest family of Protestants, numbering more than 60 million worldwide.

Today, Lutheran churches are growing fastest in Ethiopia, Tanzania, and Papua New Guinea.

Among Protestant denominations, Lutherans tend to have greater unity. For example, there are 14 Lutheran denominations in North America. In contrast, other denominational families (e.g., Reformed, Anabaptist, Baptist) have at least twice that number.

To prepare for "The Mysterious Veil," read 1 Thessalonians 4:13–18.

The Mysterious Veil

Vital spark of heavenly flame!
Quit, oh quit this mortal frame!
Trembling, hoping, lingering, flying,
Oh the pain, the bliss of dying!
Cease, fond Nature, cease thy strife
And let me languish into life!

—Alexander Pope,
"The Dying Christian to His Soul"

Lutherans begin their study of the end times with a topic that many people hate to discuss: death. The Bible describes death as a veil or a burial shroud (Isaiah 25:7). Sooner or later all people face this mysterious veil. Until Christ reappears, death remains *the* entry point for the end times.

1. What attitudes do the people you know have about death? What attitude do you have about death?

2. We prepare for major life events such as a wedding or the birth of a child. How do people prepare for death? How have you prepared for death?

Lifting the Veil

People die from famine, accidents, disease, and warfare. They die from old age. Properly speaking, these are not the primary causes of death, but what theologians have called the "instrumental" causes of death.

3. What cause of death does the Bible identify? Read Romans 5:12 and Genesis 3:17–19.

4. Medical writings describe in great detail what happens to a person at death. What information do Matthew 10:28; Luke 12:20; and Matthew 27:50 provide about death?

5. What happens after death? See Hebrews 9:27.

6. How does the Bible describe the death of unbelievers? Read Proverbs 11:7.

7. God has forgiven the sins of believers. Why then do they still die? Consult 1 Corinthians 15:50, 53–54.

8. Even though believers die, how does the Bible describe their death in 1 Thessalonians 4:13 and Revelation 14:13?

9. How does the Bible describe the attitude of believers when they face the death of a loved one? Look at John 11:32–36 and 1 Thessalonians 4:13–14.

Facing the Veil

When archaeologists uncover early human burial sites, they frequently find evidence of ritual and belief about an afterlife. For example, early graves often have red ochre (red soil used for making paint) spread about the body as a symbol of blood and life. Whether ancient or modern, every human being must struggle with how to face death.

10. Death is the great equalizer. Rich and poor, powerful and

weak, great and small—all will die. How does this knowledge affect the way you live?

11. Recall the confidence expressed in the opening poem. Describe your confidence in the face of death.

12. Mary, a member of your congregation, recently lost a family member in a sudden accident. She cannot help feeling that it was unfair for her loved one to die. She is bitterly depressed. What might you say to Mary?

Lifting the Veil for a Friend

13. The anguish over losing a loved one passes away slowly. What can you do to help someone grieving the loss of a loved one? How can your congregation help?

Comparisons

Eastern Orthodox: When people die, God judges them immediately. The righteous enter paradise; the unrighteous enter Hades. Orthodox churches reject the idea of purgatory. Based on ancient custom (to prepare people for eternity) they pray for the dead. *The Longer Catechism of the Eastern Church* states, "How have we salvation by Christ's doctrine? When we receive it with all our heart, and walk according to it. . . . How have we salvation by Christ's life? When we imitate it."

Lutheran: Death is a result of the Fall and separates body and soul. At death all souls enter heaven or hell depending on their relationship to Jesus Christ. Lutherans differ from other denominations because they emphasize that eternal salvation comes only by God's grace through faith in Christ. Whereas other denominations focus on personal goodness or holiness as preparation for eternity, Lutherans emphasize the holiness and goodness of Christ, the Savior.

Reformed: Death is a result of the Fall and separates body and soul. At death all souls enter heaven or hell depending on their predestination to grace. The Westminster Confession of Faith states, "[Those who] truly believe in the Lord Jesus and love him in sincerity, and endeavoring to walk in all good conscience before him, may in this life be certainly assured that they are in a state of grace, and may rejoice in the hope of the glory of God" (chapter XVIII).

Roman Catholic: Death closes the time for accepting or rejecting God's grace. Depending on people's faith and works, they enter one of several states: (1) Unbaptized infants go to limbo; they do not suffer punishment but cannot attain the beatific vision. (2) The righteous go to purgatory, a step on the way to the beatific vision. In purgatory they make satisfaction for remaining unrighteousness. (3) The Virgin Mary, baptized infants, and some saints enter the beatific vision. (4) The utterly wicked go to hell. Roman Catholics pray for the dead to help them escape purgatory.

Anabaptist: Death is a result of the Fall and separates body and soul. The Dordrecht Confession states, "For neither Baptism, Supper, nor church-fellowship, nor any other external ceremony, can, without faith, the new birth, and a change or renewal of life, help or qualify us, that we may please God or receive any consolation or promise of salvation from Him" (Article VI).

Baptist: Death is a result of the Fall and separates body and soul. Particular Baptists, like the Reformed, teach that all souls enter either heaven or hell depending on their predestination. General Baptists teach that all souls go to heaven or hell depending on whether they have decided to accept Christ. Children who have not reached the age of accountability also go to heaven. "We believe that the blessings of salvation are made free to all by the Gospel; that it is the immediate duty of all to accept them by a cordial, penitent, and obedient faith" (New Hampshire Baptist Confession).

Wesleyan: Death is a result of the Fall and separates body and soul. At death the soul enters heaven or hell depending on whether it accepted Christ as Savior and led a holy life. John Wesley preached, "But 'without holiness no man shall see the Lord,' [Hebrews 12:14] shall see the face of God in glory. . . . Then, at length, you will see . . . the necessity of holiness in order to glory" (sermon on the New Birth).

Liberalism: Death is part of the natural order. There is no place of eternal punishment (hell) for souls after death. At death people escape the wages of sin.

Point to Remember

"We believe that Jesus died and rose again and so we believe that God will bring with Jesus those who have fallen asleep in Him." 1 Thessalonians 4:14

To prepare for "Recognize the Signs," read Revelation 13–14.

Recognize the Signs

Appear, Desire of Nations;
Thine exiles long for home.
Show in the heavens Thy promised sign;
Thou Prince and Savior, come!

—Henry Alford, "Ten Thousand Times Ten Thousand"

Throughout history, Bible readers have associated certain signs with the end of time. For example, Franciscan monks in the Middle Ages feared the coming of the Antichrist and scrutinized the actions of each new emperor or pope, wondering, "Could this one be the Antichrist?"

14. What signs of the Antichrist do people seek today?

St. John and St. Paul do state that immediately before Christ's second coming a final rebellion will occur against Him. However, as you read Revelation, remember that the primary purpose of its symbols is not to reveal the Antichrist and future world events. Revelation directs our attention to Christ and His glorious victory over all evil. The victory belongs to Christ, and the people of God share in that victory by His grace.

Good and Evil

Many turn immediately to the Book of Revelation for a description of the Antichrist—and find none! Only John's letters use the term *Antichrist.* John makes a number of points in this regard.

15. What does John say about the Antichrist? Consult 1 John 2:18–22; 4:1–3; and 2 John 7.

16. Though St. Paul does not use the term *Antichrist*, he speaks of the "man of lawlessness" who will emerge. What does Paul say about this person? See 2 Thessalonians 2:1–12.

17. In Revelation St. John saw two beasts summoned by Satan to work evil on earth. The second beast is commonly associated with the Antichrist. How does St. John describe him in Revelation 13:11–18?

18. What does the beast from the earth do?

19. Does John provide any clues as to how we might identify the beast?

20. Though people give much attention to how the Antichrist will be revealed immediately before the end, both Paul and John state that already God's people fight his spirit. What else does Paul say about warfare between believers and the powers of darkness? Turn to Ephesians 6:10–13.

21. Though the Antichrist will rage for a time on earth, what will become of him? Read Revelation 14:9–13 and 20:7–10.

Discern the Signs

Many people point to certain historical figures as the Antichrist. Some think St. John in Revelation described Nero Caesar, who perse-cuted Christians for a short period of time. The Franciscans of the

Middle Ages and the Reformers stated that the pope exhibited many marks of the Antichrist. During World War II some people identified Hitler as the Antichrist.

22. How do these historic people measure against the Bible's description of the Antichrist?

23. Is the spirit of the Antichrist active now? Provide some examples.

24. How can you at your congregation fight against the Antichrist? How can you achieve victory?

Vital Signs

The spirit of the Antichrist is a spirit that cannot abide the truth, because Satan himself is the father of lies, in whom there is no truth (John 8:44). And the Antichrist will be identified by his lying words. This week consider how you might come to a greater knowledge of the truths of Scripture and live according to them so that by God's grace you see through the lies of the Antichrist.

Comparisons

Symbolism: Eastern Orthodox, Lutherans, Reformed, Roman Catholics, and some Wesleyans have interpreted the visions of Revelation symbolically.

Literalism: Anabaptists, Baptists, and some Wesleyans have interpreted the visions of Revelation literally.

Historicism: Liberals do not treat Revelation as prophecy. They interpret Revelation as a history-bound protest against the Roman Empire. For example, many liberals think the "beast" of Revelation represents the Roman emperor Nero.

Point to Remember

"Dear children, this is the last hour; and as you have heard that the antichrist is coming, even now many antichrists have come. This is how we know it is the last hour." 1 John 2:18

To prepare for "Love His Appearing," read Matthew 24–25.

Love His Appearing

Commending those who love me to His care,
As I hope in their prayers they will commend me,
I look through the help of God to a joyous meeting
With many loved ones gone before.

—"The Creed of Abraham Lincoln"

When Jesus ascended into heaven, angels appeared to His disciples and told them that He would return (Acts 1:10–11). The early Christians lived with this expectation, yet Christ did not return during their lifetime. Today we long for His appearing and the joyous reunion of heaven.

25. Do people today have the same expectation about Christ's return as the early Christians? Explain.

26. What ideas or events do you commonly associate with Christ's return?

Glorious Appearing

When Christ first came to earth, He was born in humility at Bethlehem.

27. Compare Jesus' first coming to earth with His second coming. Consult Acts 1:9–11; Matthew 24:29–31; and Revelation 1:7.

28. People have often made predictions about Christ's return. Does the Bible provide any clues? See Matthew 24:14, 32–33, 36, 42–44; and 1 Thessalonians 5:1–6.

29. What will happen at Christ's return? Read Matthew 24:4–13, 32–34; 25:31–32; and 1 Thessalonians 4:13–18.

30. How does the Bible describe the attitude of unbelievers about Christ's return? Read Isaiah 2:12, 19; and Revelation 6:15–17.

31. In contrast, how does the Bible encourage believers with Christ's return? Consult Luke 21:27–28; Psalm 96:11–13; and Revelation 21:2–4; 22:20.

32. No one knows when Christ will return. How then can believers be ready? Look at Luke 21:34–36 and 1 Thessalonians 5:1–11.

Comforting Presence

Although parents who expect the birth of a child never know with certainty when the child will be born, they are never caught by surprise. Why?

33. Compare the wait for a child's birth to Christ's return. See 1 Thessalonians 5:3.

34. Joe, a fellow Christian and your friend, is worried that he will not be ready for Christ's return. "Jesus is coming like a thief," he says. "What will happen to me if He returns while I am preoccupied with something else or committing a sin?"

35. The Bible often compares Christ's return for His people to a bridegroom coming for His bride. Think about the weddings you have attended. Why might the Bible use this comparison?

Reveal Christ for Another

Couples fall in love, marry, and await the birth of their child. They spend months preparing for the long-expected and wonderful day when their child will be born. This next week in your devotions at home, consider how you are ready for the coming of Christ. Take stock! What hinders your readiness? What helps? Pray for God's blessings and begin to make the appropriate and necessary changes.

Comparisons

At Any Time: Eastern Orthodox, Lutherans, Roman Catholics, and some Reformed and Wesleyans expect the following signs: apostasy, worldwide preaching of the Gospel, and the appearance of the Antichrist. These churches believe that Christ could return at any time.

Watch for Specific Signs: Anabaptists and Baptists, with some Wesleyans and Reformed, expect certain identifiable signs: the rapture, seven years of tribulation, the Antichrist, the mass conversion of Jews to Christianity, a thousand-year rule, and a variety of other events based on particular interpretations.

Liberalism: Liberals do not believe Christ will return, since they deny the resurrection of the dead.

Point to Remember

"Now, brothers, about times and dates we do not need to write to you, for you know very well that the day of the Lord will come like a thief in the night." 1 Thessalonians 5:1–2

To prepare for "The Millennial Reign," read Revelation 20.

The Millennial Reign

But peaceful was the night
Wherein the Prince of Light
His reign of peace upon the earth began.

—John Milton, *"On the Morning of Christ's Nativity"*

Just as people associate the appearance of the Antichrist with the latter days, they also often think of the millennium. Revelation speaks of a thousand-year period when the followers of Christ come to life and reign with Him upon the earth.

36. Why is it important to understand how this teaching coincides with God's overall plan of salvation in Christ?

Christ Reigns Now

The millennium is a term commonly associated with the end times. The teaching about the millennial reign of Christ is found in Revelation 20:1–6.

37. What happens to Satan in this thousand-year period?

Take note! Some translations badly garble verse 4, which contains a long sentence in the original Greek. (In an effort to make this text read more like English, the translators divide it into several sentences. For a rendering closer to the Greek, see this passage in the KJV.) Verse 4 describes all God's people from heaven down to earth: (1) those on thrones, (2) the souls of the martyrs, and (3) those who refused the mark of the beast.

A second problem with some translations appears at the end of verse 4. The new life of believers is described as if it were a future event. In fact, more faithful translations show that believers enjoy new life *now* and reign with Christ *now* ("they lived and reigned with Christ," KJV).

38. St. John speaks of a "first resurrection" and a "second death." What does he mean? For help see Revelation 20:6, 14.

39. Who are the people of God, who live and reign with Christ? Consult 1 Peter 2:9–10; Revelation 1:5–6; and John 3:2.

40. What does Satan do when the thousand years are completed? Read Revelation 20:7.

John himself states in the first chapter of Revelation that people are made a kingdom through the blood of Christ. Peter also describes believers as a "holy nation." That is, by God's grace in Christ, believers on earth are made part of Christ's kingdom. They claim Christ as their King on earth and look forward to being a part of Christ's glorious kingdom in heaven. Christ rules now in the hearts and minds of His people (Colossians 1).

Peter (1 Peter 2:7–9) and John (Revelation 1:6) link the ideas of kingdom and priesthood together. That is, the authority of believers upon earth in Christ's kingdom of grace is to serve as "priests" to God.

41. In what respect do God's people reign on earth? Look at Matthew 16:17–19.

42. How should we understand the "binding" of Satan? For a hint, look at Matthew 12:24–29.

43. Millennialists place great emphasis on Jerusalem and the role of the Jewish people during the end times. Discuss what you have heard about these teachings.

What about the number 1,000? As is so often true in Revelation, this number should be interpreted as a symbol for completeness. Many Bible passages use 1,000 in this way. For example, in Psalm 50:10 the cattle on "a thousand hills" belong to God and represent His complete ownership of creation. (For general and symbolic uses of 1,000, see also Deuteronomy 7:9; 32:30; Joshua 23:10; Psalm 84:10; 90:4; 91:7; 105:8; Ecclesiastes 6:6; Isaiah 7:23; 30:17; 60:22; and 2 Peter 3:8. What parent hasn't said, "I've told you a thousand times to pick up your room!")

The complete rule of Christ symbolized by the number 1,000 extends from His first appearance and victory on the cross to the time when He comes again. During this symbolic thousand years, Satan is restricted in his activity so that the Gospel might spread freely to all peoples. At the conclusion of the "thousand years," Satan will be loosed. He will draw the nations into one last battle against Christ's people. But he and his followers will be defeated and condemned to everlasting punishment.

Kingdom Come

For a number of years now, Palestinians and Israelis have lived in the same geographical area. They call the same city, Jerusalem, a spiritual home. For Christians, too, Jerusalem bears significance as the place where Christ was crucified and rose from death.

44. Joe, a friend at a neighboring community church, insists that Jerusalem will be established as the center of Christ's millennial kingdom. How might you respond to Joe?

45. Where is the kingdom of God found on earth now? How do you individually serve in God's kingdom as a priest?

Kingdom of Priests

St. Peter and St. John call believers in Christ a kingdom of priests. This week consider prayerfully what bearing this has on your life and how you, by the grace of God in Christ, might live as a king and priest.

Comparisons

Amillennialism: Eastern Orthodox, Lutherans, Roman Catholics, and some Reformed and Wesleyans hold that Christ rules now through His church. The thousand years of Revelation 20 symbolize the present rule of Christ.

Millennialism: Anabaptists, Baptists, and some Reformed and Wesleyans hold that Christ will establish a literal thousand-year rule on earth. Postmillennialists believe Christ will return after this thousand-year period; premillennialists believe Christ will return before this thousand-year period.

Liberalism: Liberals seek to establish God's kingdom on earth through social justice and peace.

Like most Christians, Lutherans emphasize that no one knows when Christ will return. God's people should focus on proclaiming the Gospel and serving others, not speculate about what cannot be known. Lutherans also emphasize that the created order will continue to decline until Christ returns. We cannot make a heaven on earth!

Point to Remember

"[Jesus said,] 'My kingdom is not of this world.'" John 18:36

To prepare for "Judgment Day," read 2 Corinthians 5.

Judgment Day

The mighty word of this great Lord
Link body and soul together,
Both of the just and the unjust
To part no more forever.

—Michael Wigglesworth, "The Day of Doom"

As a Puritan, Michael Wigglesworth placed special emphasis on Judgment Day. The title of his poem, "The Day of Doom," shows the anxiety that many Puritans felt about the return of Christ, an anxiety still reflected in people's obsession with the end times today.

We have already learned in previous studies that Christ will return to raise the dead. Then all people will face final judgment. Many in our society would agree that they will stand before God after death and be judged.

46. What do people commonly think about the purpose of this judgment?

47. How do people think they will successfully gain favor during this judgment?

Christ, the Judge

48. Christians have always maintained that death is not the end of existence. What is yet in store for all people? Consult John 5:28–29 and 1 Thessalonians 4:16–17.

49. Many have wondered what happens to believers between the day of their death and their resurrection. Look at Luke 23:43 and 2 Corinthians 5:8 for further clarity.

50. Describe people's bodies when they rise. See Job 19:25–27.

51. Immediately following the general resurrection of all people comes Judgment Day. Jesus Himself spoke of this event in Matthew 25:31–46. Who will judge all people?

52. How are people judged?

53. What sentence is passed and what are the various fates of those judged?

54. A vast difference exists between the final judgment of believers and unbelievers. What causes the difference? Read John 5:24 and Romans 6:3–11.

55. Though the Gospel writers and Paul continually remind people of the final judgment on the Last Day, they also insist that even now we live under God's judgment. Consult 2 Corinthians 5:16–21. What is the judgment of God? How does this judgment affect Paul's behavior?

Reconciled by Christ

56. You are having a discussion with Mary, a co-worker, at lunch, and the discussion has been about how people get to heaven. "I try to live a good life," Mary says. "I don't hurt anyone. I'm not a criminal. Sure, I haven't always helped people like I could have, but I hope that I have done enough." How might you respond?

57. On the Last Day we will all stand before the judgment seat of Christ. But even now we hear Christ's judgment. What words of judgment are found in the services of the church? How do these words prepare people to stand before Christ?

58. In 2 Corinthians 5:16–21, Paul expressed how God's judgment in Christ changed his outlook and behavior. He no longer viewed people from a worldly point of view and considered himself an ambassador. How might you also take on the role of ambassador? How might you, by the grace of God, encourage people to stand before Christ?

Neither Judge nor Jury, but a Witness

God has not called us to condemn other people or figure out who will make it to heaven. We are witnesses, not a judge or jury. God calls us to speak His Word to the world, proclaiming His judgment of all in Christ. For those in Christ, that judgment is "not guilty." Christ paid the price for sin by His death on the cross and has reconciled God to the world.

59. How might you carry this message of reconciliation to your home? To others? What changes might it bring?

Comparisons

Traditional Christians: Christ will bodily raise the dead and finally separate the righteous and the unrighteous.

Liberalism: There is no bodily resurrection or last judgment.

Lutherans also point out that Christ will separate the righteous from the unrighteous on the basis of faith. He will also judge people's works, punishing or rewarding people according to what they have done (the Bible describes degrees of glory and punishment, e.g.,
1 Corinthians 3:10–15; Matthew 11:21–24). All the righteous will share the same bliss in heaven.

Point to Remember

"For we must all appear before the judgment seat of Christ, that each one may receive what is due him for the things done while in the body, whether good or bad." 2 Corinthians 5:10

To prepare for "Heaven or Hell?" read Revelation 21–22.

Heaven or Hell?

And the angels, all pallid and wan,
Uprising, unveiling, affirm
That the play is the tragedy, "Man,"
And its hero the Conqueror Worm.

—Edgar Allan Poe, "The Conqueror Worm"

Based on Isaiah 66:24, Poe's "The Conqueror Worm" portrays humankind's end as a tragedy. Gary Larson, in his *Far Side* comics, pictures hell as a place where Beethoven must spend eternity in a room full of accordion players. Many picture heaven as a place where people sport long robes and halos and play harps.

In the previous session we learned that at the final judgment God will take the righteous to heaven and banish the wicked to hell. Throughout history all sorts of images and ideas have been associated with heaven and hell, many of them fanciful to the point of being ridiculous.

60. Do people give any serious consideration to the existence of heaven and hell? If so, what do they commonly think these places will be like?

Tears and Eternity

61. What is hell? Consult Matthew 13:40–43; 2 Thessalonians 1:6–10; and Revelation 14:9–11.

62. God's Word describes hell as separation from God, darkness, eternal fire, the gnashing of teeth, and the second death. What messages do these descriptions of hell convey?

63. Who is condemned to hell? Why? See Matthew 13:41–42; Revelation 14:9–11; and 21:6–8.

64. Some people think that after death unbelievers suffer only for a time until their sins are paid. Then they enter heaven. Is this a biblical teaching? Look again at Revelation 14:11. Then read Luke 23:41 and Ephesians 2:8–9.

65. Where is heaven and who dwells there? What images are used to describe heaven in these passages? What do the images convey about life in heaven? Consult Isaiah 25:6–9 and Revelation 21:1–4; 22:3–5.

66. Who will enter heaven? See Revelation 7:9–17.

Hot Topics

67. One day you hear your co-worker, Joe, say, "I simply cannot believe that a loving God would send people to hell." What might you tell Joe to help him understand what the Bible teaches?

68. Jesus stated that His followers would endure all sorts of suffering and persecution for the sake of the Gospel. What are some present-day examples of suffering and persecution? How does Scripture's teaching about heaven and hell affect the way Christians might view such suffering?

69. Mary, a member at your congregation, grieves on the anniversary of her husband's death. "I keep thinking about moments we shared. I just wish we could be together again." What might you say to bring her comfort and hope?

Off the Back Burner

St. John at the close of Revelation prays, "Come, Lord Jesus" (22:20). His earnest desire, and ours, is to leave this fallen world and to enter heaven. God delays the reappearance of His Son so that others might hear the Gospel, be saved, and have a place in heaven.

70. Who do you know who needs to hear this Good News? How might you tell her/him this Good News?

Comparisons

Orthodox, Lutheran, etc.: Hell is a place of eternal torment for the unrighteous. The new heaven and new earth describe the eternal bliss of heaven.

Roman Catholic: Hell is a place of eternal torment for those who commit mortal sins. It is not the same as purgatory, the place of cleansing suffering for believers. When the kingdom of God comes in its fullness, there will be a new heaven and new earth.

Liberalism: Liberals deny that hell exists. Some believe in a place or state of bliss after death.

Point to Remember

"He will wipe every tear from their eyes. There will be no more death or mourning or crying or pain, for the old order of things has passed away." Revelation 21:4

Leader Guide

Leaders, please note the different abilities of your class members. Some will easily find the Bible passages listed in this study. Others will struggle. To make participation easier, team up members of the class. For example, if a question asks you to look up several passages, assign one passage to one group, the second to another, and so on. Divide up the work! Let participants present the different answers they discover.

Each topic is divided into four easy-to-use sections.

Focus: introduces key concepts that will be discovered.

Inform: guides the participants into Scripture to uncover truths concerning a doctrine.

Connect: enables participants to apply what is learned in Scripture to their lives and provides them an opportunity to formulate and articulate a defense of a key doctrine.

Vision: provides participants with practical suggestions for extending the theme of the lesson out of the classroom and into the world.

The Mysterious Veil

Have students prepare for this topic by reading 1 Thessalonians 4:13–18.

Objectives

By the power of the Holy Spirit working through God's Word, participants will (1) describe what the Bible teaches about temporal death, (2) examine how one's attitude about death affects the way one lives, (3) rejoice that Jesus has altered the nature of temporal death for believers, and (4) determine how they and their congregation might help the bereaved.

Opening Worship

Any Bible study about death needs to emphasize how Christ came to save us and conquered death. To introduce this emphasis, read the passage by Alexander Pope and then open with prayer.

Focus

1 and 2. Read aloud the paragraph and then allow time for participants to discuss their answers to the questions. Answers will vary.

Lifting the Veil (Inform)

3. The primary cause of death is sin. When Adam and Eve rebelled against God, they died spiritually. Their natural love, trust, and obedience of God were immediately replaced by hatred, fear, and rebellion. They eventually died physically (temporal death) and returned to dust. All creation was cursed and subject to death and decay as a result of their sin.

4. Death is not the end of existence. Rather, death is separation of the soul from the body. Jesus shows this by distinguishing between the destruction of the body and the soul. Also, the Gospel writers describe Jesus' death as the yielding of His spirit.

5. The Hindu religion teaches that people are reincarnated after

death, living out successive lives. In contrast, the Bible states that people die only once and then face final judgment.

6. Some believe that all people who die will enjoy a blessed afterlife, that God accepts everyone. However, Proverbs describes the death of unbelievers as the loss of all hope.

7. Christ forgives the sin of believers. Yet in God's description of salvation, there is a "now and not yet" aspect to the lives of believers. That is, God declares them righteous, forgiven children for Christ's sake, yet they still will experience suffering and death. The last enemy of God's people, which Christ will subdue on Judgment Day, is death itself. Paul looks forward to a time when the mortal bodies of believers will be given up for immortal and glorious ones.

8. In contrast to the death of unbelievers, the death of believers is described by God's Word with gentle words: the dead "fall asleep" (1 Thessalonians 4:13) and are "blessed" (Revelation 14:13). Far from being the final and irretrievable loss of all that is held dear, the death of believers is a homecoming, the moment when they will be completely released from all sorrow and suffering and glorified with the saints in heaven.

9. Because we live in the "now and not yet" and because we still face death, we weep at the loss of loved ones, even as we rejoice in the hope of a blessed reunion in heaven. Note well, for example, the emotions of Jesus at the grave of Lazarus. Jesus knew that in a few moments Lazarus would be alive and restored to his family, yet He wept at the suffering of Mary and Martha. Similarly, Paul does not tell the Thessalonians to cease their sorrowing. Instead, he emphasizes that in the midst of their sorrow, they have hope.

Facing the Veil (Connect)

10. Answers will vary. This question provides opportunity for Law applications in the Bible study. In the final analysis, only short-sighted, foolish, or ignorant people take no thought of the day of their death. Reexamine your priorities and attitudes about material things, family, work, and goals. Above all, think not only of temporal things, but also eternal things and your need for Christ.

11. Based on the poem excerpt and other studied passages, discuss the exact nature of a believer's hope when facing death: new life in Christ.

12. Answers will vary. We learn from the Book of Job that from a worldly point of view, suffering and death may seem unfair. Evil, by its very nature, does not operate by just principles. That is, there are no guarantees that "bad" people die young and "good" people live to a ripe old age. So we might well sympathize with Mary when she, like Job, expresses how unfair she thinks it is for a loved one to die unexpectedly and prematurely (Job 1:18–19). But also like Job (19:25–27), Mary can be encouraged to trust Christ as the Redeemer. In the midst of sorrow, God's Word assures her of a blessed reunion in heaven.

Lifting the Veil for a Friend (Vision)

13. Consider how you and your congregation minister to the bereaved. "Carry each other's burdens, and in this way you fulfill the law of Christ" (Galatians 6:2).

Recognize the Signs

Objectives

By the power of the Holy Spirit working through God's Word, participants will (1) describe what the Bible teaches about the Antichrist, (2) consider how they as God's people fight against evil, (3) recognize the symbolic character of Revelation, and (4) give thanks that Christ has won the victory for the people of God as they fight against evil.

Opening Worship

To introduce the topic for today, remind participants that although they will be searching the Scriptures for information concerning the Antichrist, Christ has been glorified and rules powerfully over all. Then sing the first and last stanzas of "Crown Him with Many Crowns" (*LW* 278; *TLH* 341).

Focus

14. Read aloud the opening paragraph. Then allow participants time to discuss the question. Answers will vary.

Good and Evil (Inform)

15. While affirming that the Antichrist will indeed come, John states that already many "antichrists" have appeared and that the spirit of the Antichrist is already active in this "last hour" (1 John 2:18). John identifies an antichrist as anyone who "went out from us" (i.e., left Christ's church, 1 John 2:19) and denied that Jesus is the Christ (1 John 2:22) or that He had come "in the flesh" (1 John 4:2–3 and 2 John 7; John is combating an early heresy called gnosticism).

From these passages we may conclude that (1) the latter days or "end times" already existed in John's day and in fact extend from the day of Pentecost to Judgment Day, (2) throughout these end times the spirit of the Antichrist leads people to deny the person of Christ, and (3) the Antichrist is still to come.

16. Paul speaks of a person who will exalt himself above God and will in fact claim to be God (v. 4). Though Paul calls this person the "man of lawlessness" and not the Antichrist, most would see these as different names for the same person. This person will appear immediately before Christ returns (v. 3) and will lead a rebellion against Christ and His people (v. 4). This person is not yet active in power because he is held in check. When God's purposes are accomplished (that is, when the Gospel has been preached to all nations, Matthew 24:14), then the man of lawlessness will be let loose to do the work of Satan (v. 9). He will openly reveal himself in opposition to Christ, performing counterfeit miracles that will deceive all who do not love the truth (vv. 9–10). But his rebellion will be short-lived, and he will be destroyed (v. 8).

17. John states that this beast, an agent of Satan, has two horns like the lamb but speaks like the dragon. Note the symbolism! In Revelation "horn" symbolizes power. The person claims to have the power and authority of the Lamb (Christ), but he speaks like the dragon (Satan). He is Satan's agent masquerading as Christ. He is truly a "false Christ," which is what "Antichrist" means.

18. He, like Paul's man of lawlessness, performs miracles to deceive. The man of lawlessness causes all who do not worship Satan's first agent, the beast from the sea, to be killed. In a travesty of Revelation 7:3, where God places a mark upon His people to show that they belong to Him, this beast forces a mark to be placed on his followers and causes economic hardship for all who do not receive this mark.

19. The beast has a mark, the number of his name, 666. In ancient times, letters served as numbers (e.g., a = 1, b = 2). In other words, if one were to take the beast's name, assign a number to every letter according to its order in the alphabet, and then add all those numbers together, the sum would be 666. Since all attempts to identify the beast in this way have failed, many interpret the number symbolically. For example, seven was considered a divine number. So if 777 would be a number of the Holy Trinity, then 666 is a counterfeit of that name.

The beast cannot be identified by outward appearance. He appears like a lamb! But his words betray him. He "speaks like the dragon." Just as Christians identify "antichrists" today by their false teachings, they will identify *the* Antichrist by his false words.

20. Remember that throughout history God's people have fought

against the forces of evil by His power and grace. You are now involved in warfare. Christ gives you the equipment to carry on this fight. Christ's victory on the cross assures you of your victory over sin, death, and the power of Satan.

21. The biblical authors maintain that Satan's final rebellion will be short and end in defeat. He, the beasts, and all their followers will be cast into hell.

Discern the Signs (Connect)

22. Hitler, though truly an evil person, does not fit the description of St. John or St. Paul. His primary mission was not to rebel against Christ by masquerading as Christ and putting Christians to death. Nero Caesar did indeed persecute Christians. He was responsible for the deaths of Peter and Paul, among others, and his name, in Hebrew and slightly misspelled (!), adds up to 666. Yet though he might properly be thought of as an antichrist, he falls short of the Antichrist portrayed by the biblical authors. The medieval popes, inasmuch as they held power in the church and caused people to trust in their own good works rather than Christ, seemed likely candidates. Agreeing with the conclusions of the medieval Franciscans, the Lutheran Confessions state, "our consciences are sufficiently excused; for the errors of the kingdom of the Pope are manifest. And Scripture with its entire voice exclaims that these errors are a teaching of demons and of Antichrist" ("Of the Power and Primacy of the Pope," *Triglotta*, p. 517). But the final assault of the Antichrist has not yet appeared.

23. The spirit of the Antichrist was active in St. John's day and remains active today. For example, one thinks of the so-called "Jesus Seminar." This group of scholars, many of whom are ordained ministers, maintains that Jesus was only a man and did not rise from the dead. Such people serve the spirit of the Antichrist.

24. On the cross Jesus defeated Satan and his agents. Christ has given His people the victory. Even though you may suffer for the sake of the Gospel and Christ (as has been true always for the people of God!), you have victory. Read Revelation 12:10–12 and Romans 8:31–39. God's victory belongs to you!

The proclamation of the Gospel fights against evil. The moment a person comes to faith, Christ's victory snatches that person away from the powers of darkness. The moment a person dies in the faith, he or she enters glory and celebrates Christ's victory. Allow time for people to provide examples of that victory in their congregation, home, or workplace.

Vital Signs (Vision)

Read the paragraph and commend the activity to participants. Remind them of Jesus' promise to lead them into all truth (John 14:16–17), vital faith, and life so that they will not be deceived by the lies of Satan.

Love His Appearing

Objectives

By the power of the Holy Spirit working through God's Word, participants will (1) describe what the Bible teaches about Christ's second coming, (2) share how believers can be ready for Christ's coming, and (3) rejoice in the certainty of Christ's return for His people.

Opening Worship

To introduce the topic of Christ's return, read Matthew 25:1–13. Then sing stanza 1 of "Wake, Awake, for Night Is Flying" (*LW* 177).

Focus

25. Answers may vary.

26. All sorts of events are associated with Christ's return, some biblical and others not. Don't get bogged down with too many details at this point. Remind participants of the goals of this lesson and that ideas such as the millennium will be discussed in later lessons.

Glorious Appearing (Inform)

27. In contrast to His humble birth at Bethlehem, Christ's second coming will be glorious and evident to all. The passages affirm that He will come in the clouds, attended by His holy angels. All those alive at the time will see Him with their own eyes. Throughout history individuals have insisted that Christ has already returned. The Jehovah's Witnesses, for example, believe that Christ returned in 1914. But according to Scripture, His return will be an event that no one will miss.

28. Jesus taught emphatically about this event. Though signs provide evidence that Christ will return soon, no one, not even the angels of heaven, knows the exact time (Matthew 24:36, 42–44). On the contrary, Paul states that the day will come like a thief, when people do not expect it (1 Thessalonians 5:1–3). So any prediction about

the year of Christ's return does not come from the Bible or Christ. When the Gospel has been proclaimed to all (Matthew 24:14), that is, after the gracious will of God in Christ has accomplished its purpose, Christ will return. Beyond that, nothing more can be stated.

29. Among the signs that Christ's return is imminent (Matthew 24:33) are the persecution of believers and general apostasy (Matthew 24:4–13). Some interpreters have insisted that the fig tree represents Israel, which reemerged as a nation in 1948, marking the last generation before Christ returns (Matthew 24:32–34). Remind participants that a biblical generation (40 years) came and went in 1988 and Christ did not return. The blossoming fig tree is a metaphor, not the sign itself, for Christ's return. In other words, just as a blossoming fig tree tells people that summer is near, so also persecution and apostasy (the "these things" of verse 33) will tell people that Christ's return is near. The disciples' own generation would see these things "begin to happen" (a better translation of the Greek in verse 34).

At Christ's return, all the dead will rise and then all people together will stand before Him for judgment (Matthew 25:31–32). Emphasize that the Bible nowhere separates Christ's return from the resurrection of the dead and final judgment. In fact, Paul explicitly states that believers who have died will be among the first to meet Christ at His second coming (1 Thessalonians 4:13–18).

As popularized in LaHaye and Jenkins's *Left Behind* series, some people think that Christ will return only for believers alive at that time so they might escape a period of great tribulation upon earth. After that, Christ will establish a glorious earthly millennial kingdom in Jerusalem. They assert that after this millennial kingdom has run its course (a thousand years) and after a final battle (Armageddon), the dead will rise and final judgment will take place.

30. For unbelievers Christ's return will be a time of great fear. His return ushers in their final condemnation. LaHaye and Jenkins's teaching is dangerous because it tells people they will have a second chance to repent, after the rapture. But the time to repent is now!

31. In contrast to the utter terror of unbelievers, believers are called to lift up their heads and rejoice at Christ's return (Luke 21:27–28). His return announces their final deliverance from all evil and suffering and a blessed union with Christ in heaven (Psalm 96:11–13; Revelation 21:2–4). Far from fearing this day, believers in Christ pray for His return to come quickly (Revelation 22:20).

32. The Bible compares people who have no faith in Christ and

whose worries and desires do not extend beyond this world to people who are drunk and asleep. Christ's unexpected return will indeed take them by surprise. But those who have faith in Christ's forgiveness are always ready for Christ's return. Though they don't know the time, they expect Christ's return, for they place their hope and trust in Him (1 Thessalonians 5:9–11).

Comforting Presence (Connect)

33. Answers will vary. Paul compares Christ's coming to the suddenness of a pregnant woman's labor (1 Thessalonians 5:3). Imagine a woman who is completely and utterly surprised when she goes into labor! No, she would not have known the exact time, but surely she would know she was pregnant and that labor was imminent. Christ's return will take many by surprise.

To make the point positively, just as godly parents prepare for and look forward to the day of a child's birth, so too believers prepare for and look forward to Christ's second coming. No, they do not know the exact time, but they are not surprised when it comes because they live in daily expectation of its arrival, for it marks their deliverance from evil and entry into heaven.

34. If Joe assesses his readiness to meet Christ on the basis of his own good behavior, then he has good reason to worry. No person can be ready for Christ's return if his or her own behavior is the standard of readiness. Only the rejection of God's forgiveness in Christ— unbelief— makes a person unprepared for Christ's return. Moreover, if Joe becomes so preoccupied with worldly matters that he no longer cares about forgiveness of sins or comes to hear the Gospel and receive the Sacrament, then he will have good reason to worry. In such a state a person's faith is at risk.

Tell Joe that the fact he is concerned about his readiness shows his faith is active. A complete unbeliever won't care at all! Remind Joe that God has forgiven all sins in Christ. No sin, even one Joe might be committing at the moment of Christ's return, is so "terrible" that it has not already been forgiven at the cross. Comfort Joe in the fact that God does not desire to catch him by surprise in order to condemn him (1 Thessalonians 5:9).

35. God's people have joy at Christ's return. The joy and fulfillment of attending a wedding on earth are but a small foretaste of the joy and fulfillment of hope believers will have at Christ's return.

Reveal Christ for Another (Vision)

Encourage participants to spend time this week focusing on their own readiness. Emphasize again that whatever would drive us from faith in Christ would make us unprepared for Christ. Conversely, whatever strengthens faith—such as the reading of God's Word in family and private devotions, attending regularly the services of God's Word, and receiving the Sacrament—makes us ready.

The Millennial Reign

Objectives

By the power of the Holy Spirit working through God's Word, participants will (1) describe what the Bible teaches about the millennium, (2) identify what the Bible teaches concerning Christ's reign now in the kingdom of grace, (3) affirm their own calling as "priests" in Christ's kingdom on earth, and (4) give thanks that Christ has made all believers part of His kingdom.

Opening Worship

To introduce the topic for today, sing stanzas 1 and 4 of "Jesus Shall Reign" (*LW* 312; *TLH* 511).

Focus

We have saved the topic of the millennium until now because it is one of the most controversial. Begin this topic by reminding people about the symbolic character of Revelation. For example, the Antichrist is a beast and Satan (a spirit) is a red dragon. Christ (God and man) is a lamb with seven horns and seven eyes!

36. Read the paragraph and let participants respond. Remind them that a thousand-year reign of Christ is mentioned only in Revelation.

Christ Reigns Now (Inform)

"Millennium" is a label attached to the biblical teaching that Christ's people will reign on earth for one thousand years. This teaching is found only in Revelation. Though many other places in the Bible have much to say about the reign of Christ, nowhere else is a thousand-year period connected to it. Having said that, it will become very important for us to let the clear teachings of Scripture about the kingdom of Christ and the reign of God's people help us interpret what Revelation says about the millennium.

37. Satan is bound in the abyss so that he cannot deceive the

nations. Evidence of Christ's rule was manifest during His earthly ministry when He cast out demons. Whereas before Christ's appearing there were comparatively few believers, today millions confess Christ as their Savior. Satan is indeed bound and cannot deceive the nations as he once did.

38. John states that the "second death" has no power over the people of God, who took part in the "first resurrection" (20:6). A few verses later (20:14) he tells us precisely what the second death is—hell. The existence of a second death implies the existence of a first, but St. John nowhere mentions this. However, in light of what we discovered in session 1, the first death is the physical/spiritual death caused by sin.

In a like manner, the "first resurrection" implies the existence of a second, also not mentioned elsewhere in Revelation. To complicate matters, St. John does not give us details concerning what the first resurrection entails. Some think there will be two bodily resurrections on the basis of this passage, yet the rest of Scripture only speaks of one (discussed in greater detail in the next session). However, the Bible does speak of people dead in sin rising to new life in Christ (John 5:25; Romans 6:4). This we need to understand as the first resurrection, and the unmentioned second resurrection is the rising of the body at the Last Day.

In summary, St. John states that the second death (hell) has no power over those who take part in the first resurrection (who are given new life in Christ).

39. St. John tells us that when Satan is bound, those who sit on thrones to judge for this period are the souls who suffer martyrdom ("beheaded because of their testimony for Jesus") and who do not worship the beast (the Antichrist). They come to life to reign with Christ in heaven.

40. At the conclusion of the thousand years, Satan is let loose for a short time, during which he goes out to deceive the nations in such a way that they unite to war against God's people. But just as these nations surround God's people, God's judging fire falls from heaven and Satan, together with his followers, is cast into hell.

41. Christ Himself gave this authority to reign to the disciples in Matthew 16:17–19. Christ sent them on His behalf to announce the forgiveness of sins in His name, exercising His authority in the kingdom of grace (Christ's kingdom upon earth). This authority extends to all Christ's disciples.

Much erroneous thinking about the millennium arises from unclear thinking about the kingdom of grace and the kingdom of glory. Make sure participants clearly understand these two ways of talking about Christ's kingdom. What distinguishes God's people from others is that they become part of the kingdom of grace when they are "born again" through Baptism (John 3:3). In the kingdom of grace believers still fight against sin and evil on earth and await their final victory over death. The faithful become part of the kingdom of glory after death. In the kingdom of glory the saints no longer battle evil or are subject to death.

42. When Satan is loosed in Revelation, he immediately goes out to deceive the nations so that they war against God's people. Therefore, his binding must mean that during the millennium he will not be able to deceive people as he did before the death and resurrection of Christ.

The only other place where reference is made to the binding of Satan is in a saying of Jesus (Matthew 12:24–29; Mark 3:23–27; Luke 11:17–22), and here the reference is indirect. In this passage Jesus described His casting out of demons as "binding" the strong man. Jesus' explanation (alongside the image in Revelation) enables us to best interpret Satan's binding as a restriction of his activity. Though he does indeed "prowl around like a roaring lion looking for someone to devour" (1 Peter 5:8), during the time of the millennium he cannot deceive the nations and lead them in open warfare against God's people as he will after he is loosed.

43. Millennialists disagree widely. For example, some believe that during the millennium Christ will reign visibly and powerfully upon earth from Israel for a thousand years. That is, the millennium is viewed not only as a spiritual but also as a politically powerful reign of Christ. Accompanying this view is the notion that Jewish people will be part of this kingdom, a heaven upon earth, and that Gentiles will be indirect recipients of the Jewish blessings. Passages such as Isaiah 2:2–5 are used to substantiate this view.

But in Isaiah 2:2–5, the "mountain of the LORD's temple" should be understood not as the future and literal raising of the temple mount in Jerusalem, but rather as a figure of speech denoting the reign of God (for which "mountain" is a metaphor), which extends from His covenant of grace (the focus of which was the temple) to all people. The notion that Christ will establish a glorious and politically powerful kingdom on earth contradicts what Jesus says about His kingdom in John 18:36: "My kingdom is not of this world."

Alternatively, Scripture makes clear that believers in Christ have been raised to new life (the "first resurrection") and become part of His kingdom. The authority Christians exercise is the authority of Christ to forgive sins. Against this kingdom, the church, the gates of hell will not prevail (see Matthew 16:17–19).

Kingdom Come (Connect)

44. The information to correctly answer the question has been given previously. Allow time for participants to frame their own response. People like Joe often imagine that God has plans for the Jewish nation irrespective of what Christ accomplished on the cross. Share in the discussion how Christ reigns now in the midst of and through His people.

45. Note that in the New Testament, after Christ establishes the church, the kingdom language begins to disappear from Christian preaching. The disciples understood that Christ's reign is not bound by geography or restricted to one group of people (Israelites). Though Christ intercedes for us at the right hand of the Father, His kingdom is found on earth wherever the Gospel is proclaimed and the Sacraments are rightly administered. Lead participants to see the importance of their own witness for Christ. In proclaiming Christ's forgiveness, they share Christ with the world.

Kingdom of Priests (Vision)

Read the paragraph and prayerfully discuss how these teachings affect your life today.

Judgment Day

Objectives

By the power of the Holy Spirit working through God's Word, participants will (1) describe what the Bible teaches about the resurrection of the dead and the final judgment, (2) confess how as believers in Christ they are ready to stand before God, and (3) rejoice that in Christ believers are righteous before God.

Opening Worship

To introduce the topic for this session, sing the first two stanzas of "Jesus, Your Blood and Righteousness" (*LW* 362; *TLH* 371).

Focus

Have someone read aloud the paragraphs. Then take a few moments to answer the questions.

46. Answers will vary.

47. Many people believe that as long as the "good" qualities and deeds of a person outweigh the "bad," God will grant entrance into heaven. This view, however, ignores God's holiness and justice. From a worldly point of view, differences indeed exist among the moral qualities of individuals. It appears that some people are not as "bad" as others. But God demands absolute perfection for those who make their own personal behavior the standard by which He will judge them (Matthew 5:48).

Christ, the Judge (Inform)

By God's power when Christ returns, all the dead will rise and stand before the judgment seat of God. The Bible nowhere separates the second coming of Christ and the resurrection of the dead. On the contrary, they happen in immediate succession with no intervening period of tribulation or millennial kingdom, as some have proposed.

48. In physical death the soul separates from the body. This has caused people to ask what becomes of the soul separated from the

body until they are reunited at the resurrection—the so-called intermediate state of the souls. The Bible shows that the souls of those who die in the faith go immediately to be with Christ in a blessed state. Jesus assured the thief on the cross that "today" he would be in paradise. Paul anticipated going to be with the Lord immediately at his death. In Revelation John sees visions of the souls of the blessed in heaven, praising God and awaiting the final judgment and consummation of all things (Revelation 7:9–17 and 6:9–11).

49. Scripture teaches that the souls of the departed go immediately to a state of bliss or torment. Nowhere does the Bible support the idea that the souls of people wander about on earth as "ghosts" or that they have the ability to communicate with the living either immediately or through medians. Rather, the Bible connects all such phenomena to demonic activity. If someone asks about the appearance of Samuel to Saul in 1 Samuel 28, you might share that some theologians commonly interpret this passage either as a trick of Satan or as a truly exceptional event by which God sent Samuel to proclaim His judgment upon Saul. Matthew 27:51–53 shows another exception, by which God illustrated the significance of Jesus' death and resurrection.

Concerning the souls of unbelievers, the few references in Scripture lead us to believe that those in torment await their final judgment and condemnation in hell. See also Luke 16:19–31 and 1 Peter 3:19.

50. By the power of God all people will rise in their own physical bodies, being recognizable to themselves and others. It matters not to the divine power of God that bodies over time decay, turn to dust, and are scattered. All will hear the voice of Christ, which will bring the dead to life.

51. The clear teaching of this parable is that Christ will come to judge all.

52. People will be judged on the basis of their deeds. The difference between the sheep and the goats is that the sheep are covered by the righteousness of Christ won on the cross. Their sin has been removed from them as far as the east is from the west, and God remembers their sin no more (Psalm 103:12; Jeremiah 31:34). In other words, the difference between the sheep and the goats is not that the sheep are less sinful than the goats. Rather, by faith the sheep cling to God's forgiveness in Christ. Christ, their judge, sees and remembers only their good deeds when He looks upon them.

53. Christ will banish unbelievers to everlasting punishment and torment in hell. Christ brings believers into the blessings of eternal life in heaven. If someone asks about the relation between judgment passed upon a person at the time of temporal death and the universal judgment of all after the resurrection, explain that universal judgment is a public proclamation of the judgment passed at death.

54. Take time to make this point absolutely clear. There is no "balance" that tips on the side of good deeds that outweigh the bad. All are sinful before God (Romans 3:23). Faith in Christ makes all the difference. When a person comes to faith, he or she escapes judgment at that moment (John 5:24). At Baptism, Christ's death becomes their death (Romans 6:3–11). Jesus paid for their sins on the cross. No condemnation awaits them (Romans 8:1).

55. Scripture makes clear that already in Christ, God has executed His judgment, for which the Last Day is a public proclamation. He no longer holds their sin against His people. Just as an ambassador is an official representative of an earthly ruler, making official statements at his bequest and on his behalf, so Paul states that he is an ambassador of God. He earnestly desires that people heed the judgment of God in Christ so that their sins are forgiven and by God's grace they receive reconciliation.

Reconciled by Christ (Connect)

56. Clarify Mary's thinking about good works. From a worldly point of view, differences indeed exist between the good deeds of individuals, such as those of a murderer and a humanitarian, and God does reward the good deeds of unbelievers (their "civil righteousness") with rewards of this world ("civil rewards"). But when it comes to heaven, nothing short of perfection is required. One must depend on Christ alone!

57. In the Absolution, the pastor bestows the forgiveness of sins on behalf of Christ. At the Lord's Supper, Christ Himself gives us His body and blood with the bread and wine for our forgiveness. These means prepare us to stand before Christ because they strengthen our faith in His forgiveness.

58. Encourage participants to consider how God will use them to call people to repentance and thus, by His grace, bring them to the point where they are ready to stand on Judgment Day, clothed in the

righteousness of Christ.

Neither Judge nor Jury, but a Witness (Vision)

59. Read the paragraph and encourage participants to devote time to consider this question. God's forgiving grace in Christ leads us to forgive the sins of others.

Heaven or Hell?

Objectives

By the power of the Holy Spirit working through God's Word, participants will (1) describe what the Bible teaches about heaven and hell, (2) confess and rejoice that God has appointed His people in Christ to eternal life in heaven, and (3) consider how they might begin to communicate a biblical understanding of these doctrines to others.

Opening Worship

To introduce the topic for this session, sing the first and last stanzas of "Jerusalem the Golden" (*LW* 309; *TLH* 613).

Focus

60. Read aloud the opening paragraphs. Then allow time for participants to discuss their answer to the questions. The Christian teaching about heaven and hell is subject to much misunderstanding at the popular and scholarly level. The popular press (Gary Larson is an example) misuse notions of heaven and hell to the extent that many people do not take them seriously. Some deny the existence of hell, just as they deny the existence of Satan.

Tears and Eternity (Inform)

61. The Bible nowhere states that hell is a place where devils with pitchforks torment humans. Christ Himself emphatically insisted upon the reality of hell. Rather than fixing the location of hell, the Bible tells us—often by using images and metaphors—what hell is like. Thus, in Matthew, Jesus describes it as a "fiery furnace" where there is "weeping and gnashing of teeth." Paul, alternatively, describes hell as a place of God's punishment and "everlasting destruction," where one is "shut out from the presence of the Lord." And John in Revelation speaks of those in hell as drinking the "wine of God's fury" and suffering everlasting torment.

62. All these images convey unending torment. Theologians often categorize the torments of hell as both the deprivation of blessings and the addition of suffering. It is the absence of God's care.

God is the source of all good things, such as the fruits of the Spirit listed in Galatians 5:22 (love, joy, peace, patience, kindness, goodness, etc.). Separation from God describes the complete absence (deprivation) of any such good. The sufferings added to people in hell include inexpressible torments, pains, and tortures of the body and soul.

63. God casts evildoers into hell. This means all who remain in a state of unbelief in Christ and therefore do not stand forgiven and clothed in His righteousness. In Revelation John describes such people as those who ultimately worship the beast (Satan) and receive his mark of ownership.

64. The traditional teaching of the Roman Catholic church is that souls of believers endure punishment for a time for their sins before going to heaven. This time is called purgatory. The passages listed, however, lead to the inescapable conclusion that a believer goes immediately at death to be with the Lord. John in Revelation states that those who suffer in punishment after death do so forever, not for a limited period of time. The thief on the cross, a last-minute believer in Christ (certainly a candidate for purgatory if it existed), was taken immediately into paradise. The teaching that believers must in some measure pay the punishment for their own sins undermines the very foundation of salvation by grace.

65. As with hell, the Bible does not fix the location of heaven. Scripture does not teach that it is in the sky somewhere or out in space. Neither is it a place where believers will necessarily sprout angelic wings and carry around harps. Though the Bible states that the saints in heaven are dressed in white robes (Revelation 7:9), here again the biblical author employs a metaphor to tell us what life in heaven will be like. The white robe is a reminder that the saints in heaven are "clothed" in the righteousness of Christ (Revelation 7:14). Isaiah describes God's glorious heavenly kingdom as a great banquet where God's people feast in His glorious presence. Note the stunning contrast! They feast on God's riches because He swallowed death! Death no longer exists there. In Revelation the glories of God's heavenly kingdom are described as a wedding whereby God unites His people to Christ's glory. Heaven is an eternal party! When pictured as a city, heaven is a place enlightened by the very glory of God and

where the people of God see Him face-to-face. These images convey the bliss that will belong to God's people. Theologians customarily speak of the glory of heaven both as the absence of all things bad, such as sorrow, sin, sickness, and death, and as the addition of perfect blessings in the very presence of God.

66. John makes clear in Revelation that those who have washed their robes "white" in the "blood of the Lamb" are fit to stand before God in heaven. This righteousness is granted to a believer at Baptism (Romans 6:1–11).

Hot Topics (Connect)

67. You might tell Joe that God certainly does not want people to suffer eternal loss and damnation in hell, and therefore He has given His own Son to suffer that loss and damnation on our behalf on the cross. But God's love never comes at the expense of His holy justice. Only the substitutionary death of Christ delivers us from the threat of hell (Romans 3:19–26).

68. Examples of how believers suffer for the sake of the Gospel will vary. A biblical understanding of heaven and hell will enable us to endure all sorts of trials and tribulations rather than give up our eternal treasure in heaven. What a believer suffers now is trivial compared to the heavenly glory. See 2 Corinthians 4:17–18.

69. Assure Mary of a reunion with her husband and all God's people in heaven, where they will celebrate together forever in the glory and goodness of God. The passage from Isaiah 25 might especially be helpful. Those blessed moments she had with her husband while he was alive—moments touched by the grace of God—are but a tiny foretaste of the glories awaiting her in heaven, where she and her late husband will banquet together in the glorious presence of God.

Off the Back Burner (Vision)

70. Read the paragraph and encourage participants to consider how they might witness to others. Remind them that Lutherans often pray, "Come, Lord Jesus. Be our guest" at meals. Encourage them to think of this prayer as anticipation of the heavenly banquet and to pray for Christ's return. Point out that for Lutherans, daily repentance and frequent Communion are preparation for Christ's reappearing.

Appendix of Lutheran Teaching

Though new twists appear almost daily, the major issues regarding the end times already existed in the sixteenth century at the time of the Lutheran Reformation. Below you will find two examples of how the first Lutherans addressed these issues. The examples will help you understand the Lutheran difference.

The Augsburg Confession of 1530

Philip Melanchthon, a lay associate of Dr. Martin Luther, wrote the Augsburg Confession to clarify for Emperor Charles V just what Lutherans believed. Melanchthon summarized Lutheran teaching from the Bible and addressed the controversies of his day. This confession remains a standard of Lutheran teaching.

Article XVII: Of Christ's Return to Judgment.

Also they [Lutheran churches] teach that *at the Consummation of the World Christ will appear for judgment,* and will raise up all the dead; He will give to the godly and elect eternal life and everlasting joys, but ungodly men and the devils He will condemn to be tormented without end.

They condemn the Anabaptists, who think that there will be an end to the punishments of condemned men and devils.

They condemn also others, who are now spreading certain Jewish opinions, that before the resurrection of the dead the godly shall take possession of the kingdom of the world, the ungodly being everywhere suppressed. (*Concordia Triglotta*, p. 51)

The Large Catechism

The Large Catechism of Dr. Martin Luther sprang from a series of sermons he preached to help his congregation understand the basic teachings of the Bible. It serves as a companion for pastors and teachers as they explain Luther's Small Catechism.

The Lord's Prayer, Second Petition. Thy kingdom come.

As we prayed in the First Petition concerning the honor and name of God that He would prevent the world from adorning its lies and wickedness with it, but cause it to be esteemed sublime and holy both in doctrine and life, so that He may be praised and magnified in us, so here we pray that His kingdom also may come. But just as the name of God is in itself holy, and we pray nevertheless that it be holy among us, so also His kingdom comes of itself, without our prayer, yet we pray nevertheless that it may come to us, that is, prevail among us and with us, so that we may be a part of those among whom His name is hallowed and His kingdom prospers.

But what is the kingdom of God? Answer: Nothing else than we learned in the Creed, that God sent His Son Jesus Christ, our Lord, into the world to redeem and deliver us from the power of the devil, and to bring us to Himself, and to govern us as a King of righteousness, life, and salvation against sin, death, and an evil conscience, for which end He has also bestowed His Holy Ghost, who is to bring these things home to us by His holy Word, and to illumine and strengthen us in the faith by His power.

Therefore we pray here in the first place that this may become effective with us, and that His name be so praised through the holy Word of God and a Christian life that both we who have accepted it may abide and daily grow therein, and that it may gain approbation and adherence among other people and proceed with power throughout the world, that many may find entrance into the Kingdom of Grace, be made partakers of redemption, being led thereto by the Holy Ghost, in order that thus we may all together remain forever in the one kingdom now begun.

For *the coming of God's kingdom to us* occurs in two ways; first, here in time through the Word and faith; and secondly, in eternity forever through revelation. Now we pray for both these things, that it may come to those who are not yet in it, and, by daily increase, to us who have received the same, and hereafter in eternal life. All this is nothing else than saying: Dear Father, we pray, give us first Thy Word, that the Gospel be preached properly throughout the world; and secondly, that it be received in faith, and work and live in us, so that through the Word and the power of the Holy Ghost Thy kingdom may prevail among us, and the kingdom of the devil be put down, that he may have no right or power over us, until at last it shall be utterly destroyed, and sin, death, and hell shall be exterminated, that we may live forever in perfect righteousness and blessedness.

From this you perceive that we pray here not for a crust of bread or a temporal, perishable good, but for an eternal inestimable treasure and everything that God Himself possesses; which is far too great for any human heart to think of desiring if He had not Himself commanded us to pray for the same. But because He is God, He also claims the honor of giving much more and more abundantly than any one can comprehend,—like an eternal, unfailing fountain, which, the more it pours forth and overflows, the more it continues to give,—and He desires nothing more earnestly of us than that we ask much and great things of Him, and again is angry if we do not ask and pray confidently.

For just as when the richest and most mighty emperor would bid a poor beggar ask whatever he might desire, and were ready to give great imperial presents, and the fool would beg only for a dish of gruel, he would be rightly considered a rogue and a scoundrel, who treated the command of his imperial majesty as a jest and sport, and was not worthy of coming into his presence: so also it is a great reproach and dishonor to God if we, to whom He offers and pledges so many unspeakable treasures, despise the same, or have not the confidence to receive them, but scarcely venture to pray for a piece of bread.

All this is the fault of the shameful unbelief which does not look to God for as much good as will satisfy the stomach, much less expects without doubt such eternal treasures of God. Therefore we must strengthen ourselves against it, and let this be our first prayer; then, indeed, we shall have all else in abundance, as Christ teaches [Matt. 6, 33]: *Seek ye first the kingdom of God and His righteousness, and all these things shall be added unto you.* For how could He allow us to suffer want and to be straitened in temporal things when He promises that which is eternal and imperishable? (*Concordia Triglotta*, pp. 710–13)

Glossary

amillennialism. The doctrine that the thousand-year reign of Christ mentioned in Revelation 20 should not be taken literally. It symbolizes the reign of Christ from His first appearing to His reappearing at the end of time.

Antichrist. Based on 1 John 2:18; 4:3, the Antichrist is one who opposes the teachings of Christ. The term is also used to describe "the lawless one" (2 Thessalonians 2:8) or beast of the earth (Revelation 13:11), a deceptive religious leader who will emerge at the end of time.

apostasy. Falling away from faith in Christ. The Bible warns that before Christ's reappearing, many will fall away (1 Timothy 4:1).

beast. According to Revelation 13:11, a deceptive religious leader who will emerge at the end of time. See also *Antichrist*.

evangelicals. In North America, *evangelical* is used to describe Protestant churches that emphasize Christ's atonement for sin as well as mission work. They generally stem from the Reformed, Baptist, and Wesleyan denominational families.

filioque. Literally, "and the Son." This phrase was added to the Nicene Creed in the West to emphasize that the Holy Spirit proceeds from the Father *and the Son*. The Eastern churches have never accepted this statement, but insist that the Spirit proceeds only from the Father.

gnosticism. An early heresy, which denied that Jesus had a physical body. John refers to gnostic teachers as "antichrists" (1 John 2:18; 4:3).

intermediate state of souls. Roman Catholics teach that when people die, their souls may go to places other than heaven or hell. Instead, they may go to limbo or purgatory. Others have held that the soul of a dead person rests in the ground until the resurrection ("soul sleep"). The Bible describes heaven and hell—at times using other terms (paradise, Abraham's bosom, Hades, Gehenna, etc.)—but does not teach about an intermediate state of souls (e.g., Luke 23:40–43).

kingdom of God. God's rule over the universe, in particular through the church. Millennialists look for a political rule of Christ on earth. Amillennialists associate the kingdom of God with the church.

millennium. Literally, a thousand-year period of time. In the Bible the number one thousand is often used symbolically; for example, the cattle on "a thousand hills" represents all creation.

postmillennialism. The doctrine that Christ will return after His church rules politically on earth for a thousand years. This view was extremely popular early in American history, but few churches still hold this view.

premillennialism. The doctrine that Christ will return to establish a thousand-year political rule on earth. This view was taught by John Nelson Darby in the nineteenth century and is popularized today through the writings of Hal Lindsey and Tim LaHaye.

rapture. A doctrine introduced by John Nelson Darby in about 1830, which states that before the millennium Christ will take up to heaven all Christians living on earth so that they will not suffer tribulation.

rationalism. A philosophical movement that is often hostile to Christianity, especially the Bible's teachings about miracles and faith. Rationalists decide what is true on the basis of human reason rather than Holy Scripture.

tribulation. Literally, distress or suffering. Based on Revelation 7:14 and other passages, millennialists anticipate a seven-year tribulation as part of end-time events. Amillennialists read these passages as describing the suffering that Christians currently experience.